LADY BIRD JOHNSON

Keeping America Green

AMERICAN HEROES

LADY BIRD JOHNSON

Keeping America Green

SNEED B. COLLARD III

Marshall Cavendish
Benchmark
New York

To Geezer Scott, Allison, and Casey

Marshall Cavendish Benchmark
99 White Plains Road
Tarrytown, New York 10591
www.marshallcavendish.us

Text copyright © 2010 by Sneed B. Collard III

Library of Congress Cataloging-in-Publication Data
Collard, Sneed B.
Lady Bird Johnson : keeping America green / by Sneed B. Collard III.
p. cm. — (American heroes)
Summary: "A juvenile biography of Lady Bird Johnson, conservationist, and First Lady"—Provided by publisher.
Includes index.
ISBN 978-0-7614-4056-7
1. Johnson, Lady Bird, 1912-2007—Juvenile literature. 2. Presidents' spouses—United States— Biography—
Juvenile literature. 3. Urban beautification—United States—Juvenile literature.
4. Roadside improvement—United States—Juvenile literature. I. Title.
E848.J64C65 2009
973.923092—dc22
[B]
2008034948

Editor: Joyce Stanton
Publisher: Michelle Bisson
Art Director: Anahid Hamparian
Series Designer: Anne Scatto
Printed in Malaysia
1 3 5 6 4 2

Images provided by Debbie Needleman, Picture Researcher, Portsmouth, NH, from the following sources:
Front cover: ©Rene Burri/Magnum Photos
Back cover: ©Bob Daemmrich/The Image Works
Pages i, 34: ©Rene Burri/Magnum Photos;
page ii: LBJ Library Photo by Robert Knudsen, #C5290-28; *page vi:* LBJ Library/Photo by ©Fred J. Maroon, #C3897-10; *page 1:* LBJ Library; *page 3:* LBJ Library Photo from Taylor Family Collection, photographer unknown, #B9742; *page 4:* LBJ Library Photo, photographer unknown, #B10809; *page 7:* Library of Congress, HABS TEX.102-KARA.V.1; *page 8(left):* LBJ Library Photo, photographer unknown, #B10740; *page 8(right):* LBJ Library Photo, photographer unknown, #B10946; *page 11:* LBJ Library Photo, photographer unknown, #B10764; *page 12:* LBJ Library Photo, photographer unknown, #B9798; *page 15:* LBJ Library Photo by Austin Statesman, #41-6-113; *page 16:* LBJ Library Photo by Austin Statesman, #41-6-84; *page 19:* LBJ Library Photo from Johnson Family Album, photographer unknown, #B6330-2; *page 20:* LBJ Library Photo by Cecil Stoughton, #1A-1-WH63; *pages 23,24:* ©Bettmann/CORBIS; *page 27:* Henry Koerner/Time & Life Pictures/Getty Images; *page 28:* LBJ Library photo by Jack Kightlinger, #B1274-16; *page 31:* LBJ Library photo by Frank Wolfe, #D914-14A; *page 33:* ©Bob Daemmrich/PhotoEdit

CONTENTS

Her entire life, Lady Bird turned to nature for comfort and inspiration.

Lady Bird Johnson

When Lady Bird Johnson was only five years old, her mother died. From that day on, Lady Bird turned to nature for comfort. Flowers, birds, and trees made her feel at home and loved. The beauty of the natural world helped Lady Bird through hard times. When she became First Lady of the United States, it also gave her a greater purpose.

Lady Bird was born on December 22, 1912, in the small town of Karnack, Texas. Her parents named her Claudia Alta Taylor. The nickname Lady Bird probably came from a nurse who said the new baby was as pretty as a lady bird beetle. The nickname stuck. Claudia would be called Lady Bird, or Bird, the rest of her life.

It is easy to see why people thought Claudia was as pretty as a lady bird beetle—and where she got her nickname.

Lady Bird's father was a rough man
who was interested mostly in money.

Lady Bird's parents both came from Alabama. They were very different. Her mother, Minnie, was born into a wealthy family. She loved nature, politics, and ideas. Lady Bird's father, Thomas Jefferson Taylor, or T. J., had only two interests—money and power. Born the son of a poor farmer, he went to Texas to make his fortune. He started a successful business. Then he went back to Alabama to marry Minnie and take her with him to Texas.

Minnie and T. J. had three children—two sons and a daughter. Lady Bird was their youngest child. Lady Bird's parents had a stormy marriage. Minnie did not fit into rural Texas. She read books. She thought that women should be allowed to vote. She picked wildflowers and posted NO HUNTING signs on her husband's land. All of these things made her an outcast in Karnack. Minnie also suffered from poor health. In 1918, when she was again pregnant, she fell down a staircase. A few days later, she died.

Lady Bird was born in this fancy, plantation-style home,
but her mother was never happy in Karnack.

T. J. was too busy making money to
have much time for Lady Bird.
He invited Lady Bird's Aunt Effie
to come and care for his daughter.

By this time, Lady Bird's father had become the richest, most powerful man in Harrison County, Texas. T. J. owned thousands of acres of land. He ran a store that sold goods to everyone in the county. He had little time for his daughter. He asked Lady Bird's Aunt Effie to come and take care of the child. A sickly person herself, Effie could hardly keep up with an active young girl. Lady Bird learned to take care of herself. She spent hours reading, took boat rides on nearby Caddo Lake, and explored the woods around Karnack.

By the time she finished high school, Lady Bird wanted out of Karnack. She talked her father into letting her attend St. Mary's, a junior college in Dallas. Afterward, she went to the University of Texas in Austin. In the 1930s, women weren't supposed to want careers. They were supposed to marry and have children. But Lady Bird wanted more out of life. She studied history and journalism. Journalism, she thought, would give her a chance to see and learn about the world.

Then she met a man named Lyndon B. Johnson.

College life offered Lady Bird a freedom she had never known before. She didn't count on meeting Lyndon Johnson.

Lady Bird and Lyndon married only a few weeks after their first date.

Lyndon Baines Johnson worked for a Texas congressman. At six feet three, Lyndon was a fine figure of a man. Right away, Lady Bird liked him. In many ways, he was like her father. He had grown up poor but was determined to make something of himself. "He seemed on fire," Lady Bird remembered.

She could also tell that Lyndon needed her. On their first date, Lyndon asked Lady Bird to marry him. "You must be joking," she answered. But only ten weeks later, she said yes.

Lady Bird told Lyndon, "I would hate for you to go into politics." But that is exactly what Lyndon did. In 1937, he ran for a seat in Congress. Lady Bird had inherited money from her mother's family, and she gave her husband $10,000 for his campaign. Lyndon won the election, and they moved to Washington, D.C.

Lady Bird felt very out of place in the nation's capital. People made fun of her Texas accent. She didn't dress as well as other congressmen's wives. Lyndon expected her to do a lot of things, but often he didn't treat her very well. Lady Bird never complained. Instead, she worked hard to become a perfect partner for her husband.

At first, Lady Bird didn't like politics, but she became a key to Lyndon's success.

During World War II, Lady Bird's political and business skills both blossomed.

Lady Bird's real training came during World War II. When the war started, Lyndon joined the navy and was sent to fight in the Pacific. Lady Bird began running his office by herself. She entertained important guests. She learned to type and wrote thousands of letters to Lyndon's constituents back in Texas.

Lady Bird also began using business skills she had learned from her father. In 1942, she bought a radio station in Austin, Texas. The station had been losing money. With Lady Bird in charge, it began *making* money. Soon, she bought other radio and television stations.

After the war, Lyndon's star kept rising. In 1948 he was elected to the United States Senate. By then Lyndon and Lady Bird had two daughters: Lynda Bird and Luci Baines. Along with her duties as a senator's wife, Lady Bird managed to care for her daughters and her home.

In 1960, when John F. Kennedy was elected president, Lyndon became his vice president. Lyndon hated being vice president. In the Senate, he got things done. As vice president, he spent too much time just sitting around. It made him angry and depressed. Lady Bird stayed by his side and got him through these dark times.

The nation, however, was about to call on Lyndon and Lady Bird to lead.

While raising their two daughters, Lady Bird helped Lyndon survive being vice president.

*The assassination of President Kennedy shocked the United States—
and thrust Lyndon and Lady Bird into the White House.
Here, Lyndon takes the oath of office.*

On November 22, 1963, President Kennedy was assassinated. Lyndon and Lady Bird became the new president and First Lady. In those first few months, they helped the nation heal after President Kennedy's death. But they also went to work.

For many years, black people and other minorities had been treated unfairly, especially in southern states. They weren't allowed to hold many kinds of jobs. They could not eat in the same restaurants as white people. Sometimes, black people were even killed for speaking their minds. But in 1964, President Johnson signed the Civil Rights Act. This set of laws made it illegal to treat people differently because of the color of their skin.

After he won the 1964 election, Lyndon launched the Great Society programs. His goal was to improve every part of American life. His programs attacked poverty, improved education, and helped minorities to vote. They improved medical care, fought disease, and protected America's natural resources. Lady Bird especially supported the last goal. "The environment is where we all meet," she said. "It is the one thing all of us share."

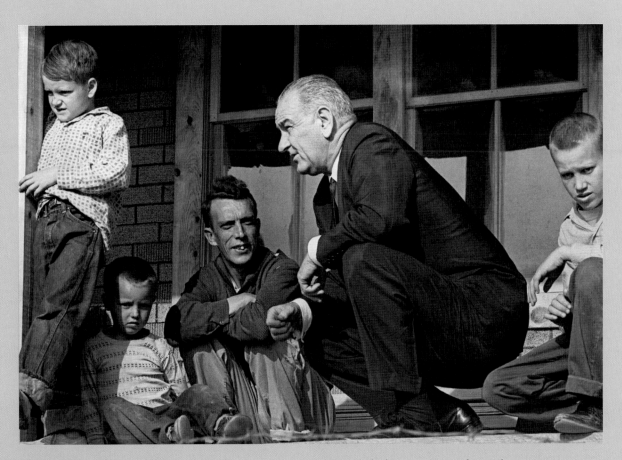

As president, Lyndon launched many programs to help poor people and minorities.

Lady Bird was the only First Lady to actively work to protect our environment.

With Lady Bird's support, Lyndon signed two hundred laws to protect our nation's environment. Lady Bird led efforts to clean up our nation's highways. She took charge of having trees, flowers, and shrubs planted all over Washington, D.C. Her work helped people everywhere care more about conservation. Unfortunately, all of Lyndon's and Lady Bird's efforts were overshadowed by a larger event—the Vietnam War.

Since the 1940s, the Vietnamese people had been fighting for independence. In 1954 the country of Vietnam was divided into two countries. South Vietnam was friendly to France and the United States. North Vietnam was tied to China and the Soviet Union. The North Vietnamese wanted to take over South Vietnam and unite the two countries.

In the early 1960s, President Kennedy had sent a small number of soldiers to help South Vietnam defend itself. When he became president, Lyndon raised troop numbers greatly—to a half *million*. As the fighting raged, hundreds and then thousands of American soldiers died in combat. The war dragged on and on, with no victory in sight. Soon, no one was talking about the Great Society programs. All eyes were turned to Vietnam.

THE TURNING POINT IN VIET NAM

TIME

THE WEEKLY NEWSMAGAZINE

VOL. 86 NO. 17

Unfortunately, the Vietnam War overshadowed many of the good programs Lyndon and Lady Bird created for our nation.

*Only Lady Bird was there to help Lyndon
through his depression over Vietnam.*

Across the United States, people protested against the war. They told President Johnson to bring our soldiers home. Lyndon was deeply troubled by the conflict but felt he couldn't simply admit defeat and pull the troops out of Vietnam. With no clear way to solve the problem, he once again sank into depression. His health began to fail. Lady Bird helped him keep going, but she was happy when he decided not to run for president in 1968.

The Johnsons spent the next four years on their ranch in Texas. They were hard years. The Vietnam War still raged. All Lyndon could do was watch. As always, Lady Bird did everything she could for Lyndon. "Without her," one person said, "he was impossible: depressed one minute, raging the next."

Lyndon died on January 22, 1973. Lady Bird, though, continued to live a long, productive life. Not surprisingly, her greatest work was for our planet.

Lyndon spent the last four years of his life on his ranch in Texas.
Lady Bird continued to watch over him.

In Austin, Lady Bird spent five years raising money to complete a ten-mile hiking and biking path along Town Lake, which was later renamed Lady Bird Lake in her honor. At the age of seventy, she opened the National Wildflower Research Center near Austin. The center works to promote native plants—those that grow naturally in each area. She said, "I want Texas to look like Texas and Vermont to look like Vermont, and every state to look like itself."

Lady Bird died in 2007. She is remembered as someone who served our nation in many ways. She also left us with an important lesson—that even during hard times, each of us can make our world a healthier, more beautiful place.

*Until her death, Lady Bird continued to work for protection
of our environment and our nation's native beauty.*

IMPORTANT DATES

1912 Born Claudia Alta Taylor on December 22 in Karnack, Texas.

1918 Mother dies; Lady Bird's care passes largely to Aunt Effie.

1934 Lady Bird earns journalism degree from the University of Texas.

1934 Marries Lyndon Baines Johnson.

1937 Lyndon wins seat in Congress.

1942 Lady Bird begins running Lyndon's congressional office during World War II.

1948 Lyndon wins seat in the United States Senate.

1960 Lyndon becomes vice president.

1963 President Kennedy is assassinated. Lyndon is sworn in as president. Lady Bird becomes First Lady.

1964 Lady Bird campaigns for Lyndon; he wins the presidency by a landslide.

1965 Lady Bird begins working on Great Society programs and conservation projects; Lyndon begins sending large numbers of troops to Vietnam.

1973 Lyndon dies.

1982 Lady Bird opens the National Wildflower Research Center near Austin, Texas.

2007 Lady Bird dies at age 94 on July 11.

WORDS TO KNOW

assassinated Murdered, usually for political reasons.

Congress A branch of the government of the United States that makes laws. Congress is made up of the Senate and the House of Representatives.

congressman A member of Congress. When people say *congressman*, they usually mean a member of the House of Representatives.

conservation The protection and wise use of the forests, rivers, minerals, and other natural resources of a country.

constituents The people a member of Congress represents in his or her home state.

depressed Sad and gloomy.

First Lady The wife of the president of the United States.

journalism The writing and publishing of articles on news and opinions in newspapers, magazines, and other media, such as the Internet.

minorities Groups of people who in number make up less than half the population of a country. Examples in the United States include African Americans, Native Americans, and Hispanics.

Senate One of the two lawmaking bodies that make up the Congress of the United States.

Vietnam A country in Southeast Asia.

TO LEARN MORE ABOUT LADY BIRD JOHNSON

WEB SITES

Lady Bird Johnson
    http://www.pbs.org/ladybird/

Lady Bird Johnson Wildflower Center
    http://www.wildflower.org/ladybird/

Lyndon Baines Johnson Library and Museum
    http://www.lbjlib.utexas.edu/johnson/archives.hom/
biographys.hom/ladybird_bio.asp

The White House
    http://www.whitehouse.gov/history/firstladies/cj36.html

BOOKS

Lady Bird Johnson: Making Our Neighborhoods Beautiful by Charnan
    Simon. Scholastic Library Publishing, 1998.

Miss Lady Bird's Wildflowers: How a First Lady Changed America by
    Kathi Appelt. HarperCollins Children's Books, 2005.

PLACES TO VISIT

Lady Bird Johnson Wildflower Center
4801 La Crosse Avenue
Austin, Texas 78739
PHONE: (512) 232-0100
WEB SITE: **http://www.wildflower.org**

LBJ Library and Museum
2313 Red River Street
Austin, Texas 78705
PHONE: (512) 721-0200
WEB SITE: **http://www.lbjlib.utexas.edu/**

Lyndon B. Johnson National Historical Park
100 Ladybird Lane
Johnson City, Texas 78636
PHONE: (830) 868-7128
WEB SITE: **http://www.nps.gov/lyjo/index.htm**

INDEX

Page numbers for illustrations are in boldface.

A NOTE ON QUOTES

MOST OF THE QUOTES in this book come from *Lady Bird: A Biography of Mrs. Johnson* by Jan Jarboe Russell (Simon & Schuster, 1999). One quotation comes from the Web site of the Lady Bird Johnson Wildflower Center (www.wildflower.org). In some cases, I did not include entire quotations but only those words that were important to what I was writing about. All of the words are Lady Bird's, however, and I have not added to or modified them.

—SNEED B. COLLARD III

ABOUT THE AUTHOR

SNEED B. COLLARD III is the author of more than fifty award-winning books for young people, including *Science Warriors*; *Wings*; *Pocket Babies*; and the four-book SCIENCE ADVENTURES series for Marshall Cavendish Benchmark. In addition to his writing, Sneed is a popular speaker and presents widely to students, teachers, and the general public. In 2006, he was selected as the Washington Post–Children's Book Guild Nonfiction Award winner for his achievements in children's writing. He is also the author of several novels for young adults, including *Dog Sense*, *Flash Point,* and *Double Eagle*. To learn more about Sneed, visit his Web site at www.sneedbcollardiii.com